Is a Consulting Career Right for You?

Your Guide to Becoming a Consultant.

Consulting is currently a popular career choice for understandable reasons. But, is consulting really the right field for you? And, if so, where do you start?

In this important Itty Bitty® book, consultant Norma Skolnik shares information regarding whether a consulting career is right for you, how to get started as a consultant and how to build a successful consulting business.

Where to Start:

- A careful examination of your own skills and interests is an excellent jumping off point.
- Ask yourself if you are expert enough in your own field to market your skills as a consultant.
- Explore the different types of consulting opportunities available in your field.
- Investigate steps to getting started.

If you are contemplating a career as a consultant and want to know what to expect and how to improve your chance of success, pick up this helpful book today.

Your Amazing Itty Bitty® Consulting Book

15 Steps to Becoming a Successful Consultant

Norma Skolnik

Published by Itty Bitty® Publishing
A subsidiary of S & P Productions, Inc.

Printed in the United States of America

Itty Bitty® Publishing
311 Main Street, Suite D
El Segundo, CA 90245
(310) 640-8885

ISBN: 978-1-931191-13-5

Stop by our Itty Bitty® website to find interesting blog entries regarding Becoming a Successful and Well Paid Consultant.

www.IttyBittyPublishing.com

nsconsulting@verizon.net

Table of Contents

.

Introduction

Consulting is an attractive alternative career option for college graduates looking for jobs or for those who've worked in industry for a number of years.

Consulting is an interesting, high-paying, high-profile field that offers the opportunity to take on a good degree of responsibility and use skills you've gained in the business or organizational world. It's also a rewarding profession that might send you all over the country or put you in touch with clients from all over the world.

Becoming a consultant may seem like a daunting prospect to those who've never been one before. But many people who have expertise in certain areas and were the experts in their field when employed, were actually consultants within their own companies, although they were called 'employees.' Once you've identified your area of knowledge and expertise and know that this is something you'd really like to do, you're on your way to becoming a consultant.

In this Itty Bitty® book, you'll find 15 key steps that should help you become a successful consultant.

Step 1
What Do You Do Best?

Consultants fill the needs of various corporations in numerous fields. To begin understanding what jobs these corporations need to fill, start by understanding what they were willing to pay you to do and why you stood out in your field. The answers to the following questions are good indicators of your readiness, what potential clients may need, and what they might hire you to provide for them.

1. What is YOUR particular area of expertise? What area is your specialty?
2. What type of work do you enjoy?
3. What made you the go-to person for certain responsibilities at your company or organization, or in your community?
4. Where is there a gap to fill or a need for your services and expertise?
5. Is there a niche where your knowledge and experience are currently needed?
6. Do you like to help people?

Where to Start

Start by assessing your experience and carefully considering what type of work you enjoy doing most, what area you know the most about, and what you excel at.

- Can you define what will make you a valuable consultant?
- Are you able to apply lessons learned in other situations to the ones you'll potentially face as a consultant?
- Are you very knowledgeable about a particular subject area?

By answering the above-listed questions and deciding if you really like working with people and helping them, you should be able to determine if you're ready to start a consulting career and become a successful consultant.

Step 2
Getting Psyched

Consulting is different from being an employee and you need to get yourself psyched to work on your own and build the necessary confidence to sell yourself; but remember that there are many advantages to working independently.

1. If you've worked in a specific area for several years, chances are you've gained enough knowledge and insight to serve as a consultant to firms that need guidance or assistance in your field.
2. You should also enjoy working with and helping people and have the confidence to do this successfully.

The following page offers some key steps to gaining confidence and appearing confident.

Tips for Getting Psyched

- When you introduce yourself, focus on your biggest accomplishment. Emphasize what makes you an expert and sets you apart from others in your field.
- Don't waste time worrying about what others might think about you. Negative self-talk can undermine your confidence. Focus on how well-qualified you are and on all the things that you do really well.
- The resume you provide and the way you look create a first impression of vital importance. When you look the part, you'll carry yourself with more confidence. Dressing well and professionally communicates that you are competent. When choosing clothing, remember to dress for the occasion and for your client's business.
- The Power of Positive Thinking was written over 50 years ago, but it's message is just as true today. Try to fill your mind with positive thoughts about your knowledge, skill and expertise. Even if you know that a potential client is in trouble, be positive about how you can help them resolve their problems.

Step 3
Different Types of Consulting

There are different types of consulting firms and consulting careers that you may want to consider when starting out in the consulting field.

1. There are large global consulting companies or small niche firms from which to choose if you decide that you'd rather go this route *vs.* doing solo consulting when getting started.
2. Working for a consulting firm can help you get your feet wet, but unless you're a full-time salaried employee, most consulting firms take a big cut of whatever the client pays.
3. Consultants who work independently are usually paid by the hour, day or project, based on commission, or on performance. Such consultants are independent contractors and not employees of the hiring organization or consulting firm.
4. You are your own boss when you're an independent consultant and you have an opportunity to build your own consulting business.

Advantages & Disadvantages of Working for Consulting Firms

- Working for a prestigious consulting firm looks impressive on your resume, provides good experience, and can help you learn the ropes about consulting.
- If you begin working for a consulting firm, whether a major or a niche company, you can always switch to independent consulting later.
- There are significant differences between a career with a major firm *vs.* one pursued in a niche consulting firm. Some differences are firm-specific, so get to know the firm under consideration. Often the reasons to choose one over the other relate to organizational traits of large and small consulting businesses—and the career characteristics inherent in each.
- Unless you're a salaried employee, niche consulting firms take a big percentage of a client's fee; however, they do provide clients and valuable experience working in niche fields.

Step 4
Research Your Field & Be Prepared

Even with many years of experience as an employee, gathering the latest information about your field and learning new skills are generally required when you become a consultant.

1. Researching your field is just as important before you engage a client as it is once you get a project assignment.
2. Research competitive rates and be sure that you are getting a good rate, as well as a fair contract.
3. Stay up to date on the latest developments, laws, publications and best practices in your chosen field. Informing potential clients of the latest developments in your field and how those developments will impact **their** business, is one of the key things that make you valuable as a consultant.

Specific Ways Consultants Prepare

- Management consultants must be skilled at conducting research and analyzing it. Research means collecting raw data from a variety of sources: the client's computers, trade associations in their industry, government agencies and surveys and market studies that you usually implement yourself.
- Regulatory consultants must be completely up-to-date and familiar with all the latest federal and state regulations and proposed legislation in their field. They, like consultants in other fields, must be prepared to research and implement all laws and regulations relevant to a client's product line. They advise on product launches, labeling and manufacturing, among other things.
- Technology consultants deal with companies in different technology fields. Their advice usually helps companies use software more efficiently and cheaply, while training employees on new software. They advise companies on project management, setting technology policies and security.
- One of the most important aspects of consulting is to be thoroughly prepared for any anticipated assignment. Never contact a client or go into a meeting or conversation with a prospective client without first finding out about their business, product line and, if possible, an understanding of what their needs and expectations are.

Step 5
Legal Considerations & Logistics of Getting Started

One of the first steps to consider in starting a consulting business is forming a limited liability company (LLC).

1. An LLC can protect you from personal liability for business decisions or actions, although the liability protection is limited. With an LLC, you're usually required to pay a fee to the state in order to file your Articles of Organization. In general, you should expect to pay about $100.00 to file.
2. 70 percent of small businesses operate as sole proprietorships. A sole proprietor owns and runs the business – there is no legal distinction between the business and the owner – which means you are held personally liable for the debts and obligations of the business.
3. Managing this and other forms of risk is an important consideration and often requires a layered approach that includes selecting the right business insurance (which clients often require before entering into an agreement) and sometimes even consulting an expert about legal obligations and the best structure for your business.

Tax and Legal Obligations

During the start-up phase, it's important to make sure that you've taken care of required legal and tax obligations.

- Be sure to put aside enough money from consulting fees so that making mandated quarterly tax payments to state and federal revenue offices is never an issue.
- You can obtain your Federal Tax ID Number in minutes by using the following online form: www.gov-tax.com.

Licenses, Certifications, DBAs

- In general, consulting does not require a license. However, depending on the area of specialization, it may be essential to obtain the right licenses and permits if required.

- When you conduct business and use a name other than your legal name, you may need to register with your state to get a DBA (Doing Business as) license. If you intend to use a trade name, then you'll need to register that name with the appropriate state agency.

- Consultants working in particular fields, including health care management or engineering, may also require industry certification before qualifying for their business licenses.

Step 6
Define Your Target Audience

Often consultants mistakenly think that by defining their expertise broadly, they'll appeal to a wider audience and attract more clients. Actually, the less specific you are, the less likely it is that clients will contact you when they need assistance in your field.

Defining your target audience should help attract clients who need help related to your area of expertise and there are significant advantages to becoming a specialized consultant. Below are some reasons to consider targeting a consulting niche:

1. Prospective clients will be more likely to seek you out for your specialized skills, knowledge and experience.
2. There's less competition in a niche area. Fewer consultants will have the specialized skills or experience to meet the needs of niche clients.
3. You can charge more in a niche area. Because of your more specialized skills and knowledge, clients are usually willing to pay more for your services.
4. It's easier to get noticed and become known as an expert in a niche, which means less marketing is needed.

Your Target Audience & Niche Consulting

- There are usually a lot of business opportunities for most niche consultants in traditional areas like management, financial, engineering, regulatory or technology consulting.
- However, once you define your target audience, you may want to specialize in the next trend or niche market that is just emerging. These can be lucrative opportunities because the market is often untapped, and not already saturated with competing consultants.
- You may want to use your expertise and interest to start or expand a highly specialized consulting business in a new niche market. Examples of some of the new niche areas that have only recently sprung up are: second career consultants, voice consultants and Green Living consultants.

Step 7
Your Deliverable is Knowledge

A consultant is hired because of his or her knowledge. Therefore, it's crucial to confidently express your knowledge in the subject area for which you were hired.

1. A client picks you to work for them because you know more than they do about your area of expertise and you should always keep that in mind.
2. This requires that you must stay current and up-to-date on all the latest information, laws and regulations relevant to your field of specialization.
3. You should also be forthright and never hesitate to be honest with clients. Deliver the knowledge accurately, even if it's something that the client may not want to hear.
4. Be prepared for the fact that the client may not always like the information that you've got to convey.
5. If you convey knowledge in a weak or ineffective way, you can undermine the value of your consulting service. Of course, you should do this as nicely as possible and offer an alternate suggestion when possible.

You Are the Expert

The effective consultant should possess functional knowledge as well as knowledge of an industry. These knowledge aspects include:

- Analytical skills, creativity, strategic and tactical leadership abilities, and the communication skills to effectively convey their knowledge.
- It's important to learn as much as you can about your client's product line and the industry it represents, as well as the laws and regulations that impact that field.
- You should also be familiar with the latest trends and competitive environment in your client's industry.
- If you're conveying information that a client may not like, be prepared to offer a suggestion about an alternate route they might be able to pursue, as opposed to just saying "no" to them.
- This ability to work with the client and offer advice is what makes a valuable consultant.

Step 8
Selling Yourself as a Consultant

The first and probably most important step in becoming a consultant is to sell yourself because this is how business is done in the consulting field. In order to sell yourself in the business world, below is a list of things you should be doing:

1. Have a terrific resume. You can't underestimate the importance of having a good resume. First impressions count, and the first impression that a potential client has of you, depends on your resume.
2. Your resume is your main chance to capture a potential client's attention. Be precise in providing information about yourself. Think of your biggest achievement(s) and highlight that on your resume.
3. You should sound and look as good as the services you offer. Sound confident about your field of knowledge and whatever you're planning to convey to your clients.
4. Remember that you are the expert in your field. Charge a good fee for your services, since people tend to equate higher cost with higher value.

Steps in Selling Yourself

- Research the marketplace and target a gap you can fill or a demand for your services in certain niche areas.
- Reach out to people in that field and tell them about your availability. Ask if they know anyone or any firm that might need your services.
- Contact companies that recently downsized their staff. Such firms often need help when they realize there's essential work or new projects that can't be completed by their downsized staff.
- Be flexible. You may have a preconceived idea about what you'd like to do as a consultant. It's best to be flexible and open-minded about what kind of consulting assignments you'll take.
- If there's a project related to your area of expertise, but not exactly on target, see if you can research it and handle it before rejecting the assignment outright.
- Messaging - You should work on refining your marketing message: what you do, for whom, and why you stand out from the competition.

Step 9
Marketing, Including Social Media

The recent rise of social media platforms has made networking and marketing your skills much easier than ever before.

1. Excellent networking and marketing tools that are currently available include blogging, writing for newsletters, maintaining Twitter, Facebook and LinkedIn profiles.
2. Using those networks is a simple and free form of advertising. Informing those in your network about your current projects and commenting on what they're working on, can help you find potential business opportunities.
3. The advantage of online social networking sites is their group features. On LinkedIn, for example, if you type "consultants" in for a "Groups" search, you'll see 1,800 different groups you can join to meet other consultants and find out about events of interest in your area.

Besides social networking, it's also critical for consultants to spend valuable in person time connecting with and marketing themselves to current and potential clients and finding out about their current needs.

Marketing Options

Many consultants mistakenly devote all their time and effort to becoming experts in their field instead of spending time obtaining clients and building their consulting businesses. The following are a few marketing ideas that can help grow your business.

- **Facebook page:** Besides your own personal page, start a free business page for your consulting practice. Use it to promote current topics and to share information.
- **Twitter:** Create an account to share your ideas. You can also share relevant stories in your field of expertise.
- **LinkedIn:** Of course you need a LinkedIn profile, but also join relevant groups or start a group of your own and organize questions, topics and in-person meetings. Connect with others on LinkedIn.
- **Website:** It's not easy to market your business without a working website. Use a variety of free web design services to give your website a professional look.
- **Blog:** There are a variety of sites where you can set up a blog. See Chapter 15.
- **Speaking Opportunities:** An excellent way of promoting yourself is to speak to an audience about a subject that you really know. This provides great credibility and generates terrific audio/video clips for your website.

Step 10
Networking to Build Your Business

As a new consultant, you should be able to generate a project or maybe several through your network of friends, past employers and colleagues. Research shows that clients use their networks to select consultants more than any other method, and they are likely to know someone who may know you. So get your address book out and start making contacts.

1. Being a consultant is dependent upon building a good reputation in your industry and selling your skills.
2. Look at your network of contacts and assess the amount of work you can quickly generate, figure out how much you'll need to make in your first year to cover expenses, plus identify who would be willing to refer clients to you.
3. Contact friends and former work colleagues and ask them if they know of firms that may need your services.
4. Consider social networking to advertise your skills and the challenge of simultaneously working and networking to build your business.

Networking Steps

- **Referrals** are a wonderful way to obtain new clients. When you've finished a consulting assignment, confirm that your client is completely satisfied, then ask for a referral. Send the client a note thanking them for their business and ask them to refer you to colleagues, friends or business associates who might need your services.
- Many consultants attend **Networking events** to discover new employment opportunities. They are a great way to meet people who may know of or offer consulting job opportunities.
- There are also other advantages these events have to offer. Consultant networking events encompass a wide variety of activities, from conferences to professional association meetings and roundtables.
- Many events include workshops or seminars with an educational, training or skills building component, or a presentation featuring a guest speaker with expertise in your field. If it's possible, you should try to speak at such an event and display your knowledge.
- Use social media platforms discussed in the previous chapter to network and market your skills and discover new job opportunities.

Step 11
Estimates & Timelines

New consultants often have little experience with setting consultant fee rates or they aren't sure what to include in a project estimate. Setting your rate and accurately estimating what is involved in a project are essential to consultant success. It's also critical to make sure that you've factored in enough hours for project follow up (e.g. client questions, project revisions, etc.)

Allow yourself enough time to do a thorough job and don't promise an unrealistic completion date because the project is urgent. Below is a sample consulting estimate format. Similar to a consulting invoice, include the following basics in your consulting estimate:

1. ESTIMATE
    Name / Company Name
    Address
    Phone and Fax
    Email & Web address
    U.S. Federal Tax Payer ID
2. CLIENT'S DETAILS
    Contact
    Company Name
    Phone
    Email

Billing & Per Project Estimates

- Billing by the Hour: Billing by the hour is relatively straightforward once you decide how much to charge. For example, in your estimate you can say that Project X may take approximately 20 hours and you'll be billing hourly for your work.
- When billing by the hour, most clients would like to see a *maximum* number of hours outlined in the estimate. For example, "Project X will be billed hourly at a rate of $100 per hour, up to a maximum of 30 hours."
- Per Project Billing: Often clients prefer per-project rates because they know what to expect.
- For example, in your estimate you can state that Project X will cost $2500. If it's a large project, it's helpful to both you and the client to break down the project cost into sub-sections so that the client can see exactly how you've arrived at the total cost.
- When billing per project, it is crucial that you outline what is and what is not included in the project. When possible, be sure to outline the project parameters in the estimate if not covered in your contract. Stipulating a minimum project fee is strongly advised.

Step 12
Pricing/Setting Consultant Fees

As a consultant, you obviously must set consulting fee rates. Consulting fees can be worked out in several ways.

1. With the following information in mind, you can determine typical consultant rates - what companies pay consultants for their hours, days and projects, and what you should charge. However, it's important that you don't undervalue yourself.
2. The figure you decide upon should include compensation for your time and compensation for your business overhead, such as travel, office expenses, etc.
3. **Consulting fee models** - The main strategy options for setting consulting fees include the following:
    a. Doubling/tripling your hourly wage
    b. Using a daily rate for consulting
    c. Using an hourly rate
    d. Setting consultant fees by the project
    e. Charging what others in your industry charge

How Do You Set Consulting Fees?

Consulting agreements establish a legal relationship between a client and a consultant, thus the terms must be clearly defined.

- **Research Competitors Within Your Industry:** Your fair market value is the basis of your consulting fee. Fair market value consists of individual value and potential value. Demand for your service should affect your price. Find out what competitors within your specific industry are paid. Use this information to arrive at your fair market value.
- **Define Your Rate Period:** Consulting rates can be set as either variable or fixed. Variable rates are based on a specific time period, such as per hour or per day. Fixed rates utilize a predefined amount that serves as the total consulting fee throughout the project. If uncertain how long a project may take to complete, utilize a variable rate.
- **Draft a Basic Consulting Agreement:** A client isn't required to pay the consulting fee until an agreement is in place. Various websites, including Entrepreneur.com, offer free consulting agreement templates. These templates define the parties in the agreement and the applicable rates. At the very least, you should have a written statement from the client that they agree to your consulting fee.

Step 13
Building a Client Base

It comes as a surprise to new consultants that their knowledge and technical skills may not be their biggest asset. Those skills are obviously required and usually help get you in the door, but building a client base and long-term client relationships are really what turn out to be your biggest assets.

1. To find clients and build a client base, the key steps for a consultant to take are deciding who your ideal clients are, what to offer them and focusing on the optimal ways to find those clients.
2. Start with questions such as: Where are the clients I want? And how can I reach them? Consider what issues they care about, events they attend, websites and blogs they visit, groups they belong to and what publications they read.
3. The answers to such questions can guide you to locating those ideal consulting clients and others whom you might not have previously considered.
4. These factors should enable you to focus on conveying what you can offer these potential clients and why they should hire you.

Steps to Obtaining Clients

To obtain clients and get your message out to them, start by asking yourself the following questions:

- What conferences and events do they attend?

- What blogs and websites do they visit?

- What publications do they read?

- What groups in your field of expertise are they part of?

These are just some of the questions that can help you reach the clients you seek.

- Once you answer these questions, determine how you can attend such events, write a similar blog, appear on one of the websites or write an article for one of those publications.
- Webinars are another great way to educate and provide valuable information to ideal clients. Done effectively, not only can you display your knowledge live during the webinar, you can present it to many people at once.
- Most webinars consist of presentation slides (e.g. Power Point) that you take attendees through. It's a great way to identify the problems prospective clients may be having, show off your knowledge, offer possible solutions, and obtain them as clients.

Step 14
Dealing with & Keeping Clients

In order to retain clients, it's essential that your client should trust you and the work you do.

1. The first step in building a good client relationship is to make sure that you understand the project.
2. Asking questions is at the core of how a consultant works, so be sure that you understand what you are being asked to do and the issues that your client is facing.
3. Never be afraid to ask for clarification—it's far better than doing something that the client doesn't want and having to redo a project.
4. Your client certainly should believe that you are able to do the job,
5. Your practice is never more stable than when your customers trust you completely to take care of them.
6. Often clients call you at the last minute with an urgent project or a major change and you'll need to adapt to this possibility since it's part of taking care of the client's needs.

Steps in Retaining Clients

Following are some other important things to keep in mind about dealing with and retaining consulting clients:

- Timely responses and good client communication are essential. Make sure that you know what the client's deadline is and that you're comfortable you can meet it.
- Clients should be able to reach you when necessary, even if they're located in different time zones.
- If you work with multiple clients, as most consultants do, you'll have to learn to balance multiple and often shifting priorities, but always make a client feel as if his/her project is important and worthy of your full attention.
- As consulting projects come and go, your income is likely to fluctuate and you need to be prepared for this.

Step 15
Newsletters, Articles and Blogging

Blogs offer an inexpensive and easy way to gain visibility for your consulting business and to interact with current and future clients as well.

1. Your blog also helps to keep your web presence current and fresh.
2. It can provide new (and keyword-rich) content that helps draw new visitors and pique the interest of repeat visitors.
3. When blogging for business, you essentially have a blank slate on which to present information about your consulting firm.
4. Your blog, like a newsletter, must be current to be valuable to clients. When your most recent post is more than a month old, then you're in trouble.
5. An editorial calendar will help you avoid this problem. Decide how many posts you'll do per week or month, and decide what general topics you'll address. If something interesting or timely comes up, feel free to change topics. The calendar also holds you accountable to a deadline.

Newsletters & Articles –

Newsletters are another great way to reach potential clients and gain visibility for your consulting business.

- If you're a regulatory consultant, for example, write about new and timely subjects regarding new or proposed regulations or legislation that potential clients want to know about.
- Controversial and newsworthy topics are usually of particular interest.
- Newsletters give the client more information at one time in newsletter stories, while also allowing them to write in and contribute to the newsletter.
- Whether in electronic or paper form, a newsletter can be the perfect vehicle for building client relationships.
- Include stories that highlight interesting business doings and industry data that your readers will find useful.
- Also include how-to tips related to your field of expertise. These helpful articles will make your newsletter valuable to readers, so they'll hang on to the newsletter for reference and be reminded of your consulting business.

You've finished. Before you go...

Tweet/share that you finished this book.

Please star rate this book.

Reviews are solid gold to writers. Please take a few minutes to give us some itty bitty feedback.

ABOUT THE AUTHOR

Norma Skolnik has over 35 years of regulatory experience working with the pharmaceutical and dietary supplement industries. She served as Director of Regulatory Affairs for the Americas for Cadbury Adams. Prior to that, she was Director of Regulatory Affairs for the Adams Division of Pfizer and Associate Director of Regulatory Affairs for the Warner-Lambert company. She also served as Director of Regulatory Affairs for Lederle Consumer Healthcare, as Associate Director of Marketed Product Support for Lederle Laboratories and as Associate Director of Regulatory Affairs for Wyeth.

Norma currently works as a regulatory consultant and also enjoys coaching those who are just starting out in the consulting field.

She can be reached at
nsconsulting@verizon.net

If you enjoyed this Itty Bitty® Book you might also enjoy

- **Your Amazing Itty Bitty® IRS Audit Prevention Book** – Nellie Williams, EA
- **Your Amazing Itty Bitty® Cancer Book** – Jacqueline Kreple
- **Your Amazing Itty Bitty® Safety Book** – Stephen Carpenter

Or many of the other Itty Bitty® Books available on line….

www.ingramcontent.com/pod-product-compliance
Lightning Source LLC
Chambersburg PA
CBHW071422200326
41520CB00014B/3534